DISTORTED REALITY

Living in the Shadows of Parental Mental Illness

Antoine D. Jackson

DISTORTED REALITY
Published by Antoine D. Jackson

Unless otherwise noted, all scriptures are from the KING JAMES
VERSION (KJV) Bible: KING
JAMES VERSION, public domain.

Details in some anecdotes and stories have been changed to protect
the identities of the persons involved.

Paperback ISBN *979 862 285 3555*
eBook ASIN *B088YGQ555*

Cover and interior design by
Sow Graphics & Publications, LLC | Detroit, Michigan
Cover image used under license from Shutterstock.com Author Photo
by Q11 Photography | Southfield, Michigan
Editing by: So It Is Written, LLC

Printed in the United States of America

What people are saying about…
DISTORTED REALITY

"As a child, who was the product of a home with a mixture of behavioral issues and physical abuse, *Distorted Reality* really hit home. The book brought to mind many of the realities that I learned to bury to survive. In retrospect, I know that many aspects of my life have been shaped by the lack of professional support to develop resilience skills during those times. Thanks for the transparency!"

– Dr. Linda Koonce, RN, FACHE
*Director, Clinical Services, Aetna Better Health of Michigan
Adjunct Faculty, A. T. Still University College of Graduate Health Studies*

"In *"Distorted Reality,"* the authors recollection and immersion into the traumatic events of his childhood demonstrate—the urgent need for more support, resources, and trained credible responders to be readily available to families struggling due to parental mental illness."

– Daniel Robertson, M.A.O.L.
Program Manager, Boys and Men of Color Initiative, Say Yes Buffalo

In *"Distorted Reality,"* Antoine Jackson pulls the covers off life, as a boy, with a mother dealing with schizophrenia. He pulls no punches in describing the graphic reality of his childhood. Gripping, and filled with the faith that now pervades his life, these pages are a needed call to action for reducing the stigma related to mental illness."

– Stephen P. Hinshaw, Ph.D.
*Professor University of California, Berkeley;
Author, "Another Kind of Madness:
A Journey through the Stigma and Hope of Mental Illness."*

"As the People Expert, I have over 30 years helping people with mental illness or those impacted by those mental challenges. The one thing I have learned is you cannot heal from a thing until you are real about it! Antoine has penned a book, that shines a light on dark spaces and with his transparency will promote Real Healing. Prepare to take a look at yourself, bias, and thoughts around this real-life enigma!"

– Dr. Sabrina "The People Expert"
*www.sabrinajackson.com
www.essentialcolors.co*

DEDICATION

To my beautiful, courageous and strong mother,
Ms. Creola Jackson.
Your strength is admirable and your wit is unmatched.
Thank you for keeping me laughing.

CONTENTS

Preface *9*

Introduction *15*

1 | A Leap Of Faith 21

2 | Fried Eggs And Bacon 25

3 | The Push.. 29

4 | November 1951 33

5 | New City, New Challenges And New Birth 39

6 | Spring 1985 43

7 | Growing Up In Mental Illness 47

8 | The First Through The Eighth 51

9 | She's Not Crazy, Just Sick 55

10 | My Saving Grace, Marie 59

11 | Mental Illness In The Black Community And Black Churches 65

12 | Faith At The Center 71

13 | Baptized Into It... 75

14 | The Age Of Accountability 79

15 | The Miseducation Of Mental Illness 83

16 | Questions.. 87

17 | The Need For Resilience 93

18 | Healng For Our Wounds 97

19 | Therapy Helps! 105

20 | Thirteen Letters 109

21 | A New Level Of Care....................................... 113

22 | Endings And New Beginnings 121

A Letter To Caregivers:...................................... 127

Epilogue: 131

Help For Mental Illness...................................... 135

Acknowledgements... 142

About The Author 146

PREFACE
STIGMA AND LANGUAGE

Mental illness crosses gender, racial, religious and social lines. It has no respect of persons, and, like a perfectly fitting glove, mental illness leaves no portion of a person's life untouched. Coming alongside mental illness is the invisible bondsmen, powerfully keeping so many in bondage and restraints. I speak of the stigma.

It is oftentimes the stigma that prohibits those facing mental illness from seeking help. If you or someone you know is experiencing mental health challenges, please contact your local community mental health organization.

There is help available. Please see a medical professional immediately. You do not have to walk this journey alone.

My inner-city, predominately black community upbringing taught me several valuable lessons. If you come from a similar background, you probably know some of these lessons. Never cross a busy intersection with headphones on. Leave space for the person parking next to you to leave the grocery basket in between vehicles. But there is one lesson I wish I was not so familiar with: the stigma that exists around mental illness in predominately black—and other minority—communities.

One of the lingering taboos in the black community is the stigma around mental illness. The stigma has been the significant reason why citizens in black and minority communities do not pursue mental health services. The fear of being exposed or, God forbid being called "crazy," has left many battling mental struggles alone. Self-medicating, hiding or suicide have been the remedies by which many have dealt with mental illness.

Sadly, in predominately black communities, mental health services are lacking in efficiency or not present at all. According to the 2016 National Survey on Drug Use and Health, the cost of care, lack of transportation, and public awareness and perceptions about behavioral healthcare are also barriers to access ("Hundreds of thousands of Michigan residents lack behavioral health treatment," 2019).

Some have attributed the decline of mental health services in black communities to the community members' refusal to utilize the services. As one who has traversed the mental health field in my hometown, I can lift up two barriers that are paramount reasons why I believe people probably do not pursue the help they need. Attitudinal and structural barriers.

The attitudinal barriers are the disrespect and disdain that persons with mental illness face from service providers. I strive to be fair and impartial. So, allow me to say that, over the last twenty years, I have seen both ends of the spectrum. I have seen staff at local clinics, hospitals and social programs give the utmost in customer service and patient care. In contrast, I have also experienced firsthand the disrespectful tone and disdain shown to individuals who seek mental health services.

The second barrier is structural. Simply put, the reason many in our minority communities do not reach out for help is because of the lack of affordable, quality and accessible service. The amount of inefficient and subpar care being offered in some communities has proven to be a barrier. I have observed firsthand how care in suburban communities differs from that in my inner-city community. The offices were cleaner and well-organized, and the efficiencies screamed, "We have money!" These two reasons, though based on my personal experience, are not exclusive to me. These disparities add to the uphill battle to overcome the real stigma surrounding mental illness.

Stigma is the process whereby labelling, stereotyping, separation, status loss and discrimination co-occur in the context of power (Link & Phelan, 2001). Principally a social phenomenon, stigma influences behavior of both *patients* and the community where they reside.

In writing our story, it was important for me to determine how best to refer to my mom and others who have schizophrenia. It is important to me that you understand that *she is not a schizophrenic*; she has schizophrenia. This small, seemingly insignificant statement has fed a lot of the stigma that exists in our communities.

Have you ever considered that a person diagnosed with breast cancer is not called a "cancer"? Instead, they are referred to as a "cancer patient" or, my favorite, "a survivor." Why do we not see mental health in this same manner? Could it be because we do not *see* mental illness? Let's face it. Mental illness is an elusive, invisible, but manifesting disease. A person with mental illness can appear fine to the naked eye, but within, be in great turmoil. Sadly, we only see them after an outburst or episode, or when their mental illness leads to harm others or themselves.

Exacerbating the issue at hand are the use of words, phrases and colloquialisms that perpetuate stigma. A quick review of social media will display some terminologies that have become—dare I say—socially acceptable, even though they are insensitive and contentious. I will probably give this disclaimer repeatedly throughout these pages, so bear with me. I am not a medical professional, nor am I claiming to be. The views and opinions expressed within are those of my personal experiences, and they are not meant to be used as professional advice, nor medical advice.

Therefore, I have made the decision to use the phraseology "patient" or "person with schizophrenia" in this writing. One of the clear lessons I have learned from my mother is that, "I am still a person." These were the five words she spoke when I visited her in a mental institution. She had refused medication and the nurse seemed to be a little ruffled by her antics.

She raised her voice and said, "Take the meds, Ms. Jackson!" To which my mom reminded her that, "Hollering was not necessary. I am still a person."

My mom's words broke me, and I immediately moved in and excused the nurse. I took the medication and spoke to my mom about the show on the television. Within a few minutes, she was taking the medication without incident.

She simply wanted to be acknowledged as a *person*.

INTRODUCTION
THINGS GET HEATED

I love the summertime in Detroit. Bike riding, walking and visits to the local parks make for a great time. The updates to the cityscape, which include the 2002 establishment of The Riverwalk, have made for increased opportunity for individuals and families to engage in outdoor activities. Taking my daughter to The Riverwalk to ride bikes or walk the trail is a welcomed highlight to our summer. Oh, how things have changed since I was a child growing up in Detroit.

In the mid-90s, the excitement for summer stemmed from being out of school. Not to mention, we had more access to recreation centers, basketball courts and community-wide programming to keep our attention, though we rarely took part in any of those formal recreation activities. We found our fun organically while playing in the yard. We played incessantly, stopping long enough to grab water, flag down the ice cream truck, or to get food.

Like most summers before, my cousins and I spent what seemed like every waking hour playing outdoors. It was often after the direction of my aunts or grandmother.

"You kids go out and play!"

Thinking back, their statement served as the benediction for us when the adults needed to have a conversation that was not suitable for our hearing. In those moments, all the kids would rush for the door. I slowly lingered behind because I had an inkling that the conversation was about my mom. Or maybe I was just nosey. Sadly, most times the conversation was about my mom—how the family could care for her needs.

The year 1995 was a monumental year for the city of Detroit and our family at-large. In March of that year, one of my aunts, whom I loved dearly, was found murdered in her home. Sadly, her name would be added to the list of one of 475 homicides that year (City of Detroit, 2016). Subsequently, my grandmother became guardian to her two young children. The population of the house grew from six people to eight. It was tight in that three-bedroom house on 32nd Street. Bickering over the bathroom and dishes left in the sink were the norm.

My grandmother was a master disciplinarian, though. She could end any disagreement with one swing of her belt, bringing order and silence to the entire house.

That summer was scorching. The heatwave meant more outside time for us kids, but it spelled disaster for some as severe storms hit the region. Not to mention the newspaper strike on July 13th made for some heated exchanges and headlines. None of that compared to the heated storm brewing in our house.

Perhaps grieving the loss of her sister, my mom seemed to experience increased incidences of schizophrenic hallucinations. Her behavior had grown to be more physical. She broke windows with bricks, tore through furniture, and destroyed dishes in the house. She had picked up the habit of carrying steak knives in her bra or somewhere else underneath her clothes, convinced that people were after her.

Then, there was my brother. He is the oldest of my mother's living children. He suffered a closed head injury at five or six years old due to a fall from a second-story window. He started to mimic mom's outburst behavior.

Though not diagnosed with schizophrenia, he lashed out in fits of rage and broke things in the house. On a few occasions, we had to call the police to restrain him and get him admitted to the psychiatric crisis center. We later learned that he was diagnosed with intermittent explosive disorder—repeated, sudden episodes of impulsive, aggressive, violent behavior or angry verbal outbursts in which you react grossly out of proportion to the situation ("Intermittent explosive disorder - Symptoms and causes," 2018). We were reaching a boiling point in the house.

One day while playing in the yard, my mom came outside, yelling my name. Confused, I ran to the back door, hoping to meet her in the kitchen. When I got there, she slapped me across my face. My light complexion immediately turned red. Overhearing the commotion in the kitchen, my grandmother came into the room.

"Why are you hitting that boy?" she yelled.

Stunned and feeling the pain of the moment, I looked at her with no words. She continued on and grabbed my shirt, pushing me up against the kitchen counter. Unconscious and zoned out, she kept pushing until my grandmother grabbed her, demanding that she turn me loose.

Still confused about the moment, I stayed clear of my mom for the rest of the day. I wrecked my brain trying to figure out what I had done wrong. My grandmother, perhaps sensing my brainstorming, reminded me that she was sick and had not been taking her meds. I accepted her answer but remained vigilant the rest of the day. Later that evening as the house prepared for bed, the outburst became loud and unbearable. Granny threatened to call the police and to have her admitted to the hospital, but that only incited mom's behavior more.

By morning, no one had slept. Mom had been up all night, yelling and screaming. By noon, probably having had enough, my grandmother called the police. I learned later that my mom had grabbed a steak knife and left for the store. The police had already arrived when she was walking up the street, talking loudly. When she saw the police car, she became more enraged. When she reached the house, she let out a cry that still haunts me to this day.

"I ain't done [expletive] to you. Why are you always calling the police on me?"

I had never heard this in her voice before and my heart broke.

She tussled with the officers and the glass bottle of Faygo® Cola fell to the ground and shattered. Her blouse tore and her bra was showing. Hoping she would settle down, my grandmother kept calling her name. She only became more incensed.

The taller white male officer said, "What is her name?" Perhaps he had not heard my grandmother yelling it.

My mom, looking him in the eyes, and with the sweetest of tones said, "Ms. Jackson." Noting the change in her tone, the officer responded in a similar tone. Before long, he had settled her down, closed up her blouse, and convinced her to get into the squad car.

They took my mom to the crisis center at the local hospital. Doctors decided to admit her after Granny made a petition that recounted her activities in the days prior. Mom would spend the better part of the summer in the hospital. We were allowed to visit her a few times, but after some time, only my grandmother and aunts visited.

Ready or not, our family had leapt into the throes of mental illness.

1 | A LEAP OF FAITH

In May of 2016, I took a leap of faith to share with the world about a person and penned my first op-ed. Though I had already published several books by that time, the moment was monumental. I swelled with enormous emotion as the opportunity was presented. At each turn, the proposition seemed too good to be true. The piece was for CNN.com, one of Turner Broadcasting System's online brands. The internationally known news outlet that covers all things politics, world news, health and more wanted to highlight *our story*.

A few months prior, a CNN producer learned of our story after hearing me speak to students in Detroit. She reached out to offer the opportunity to share via their signature *Impact Your World* web series. The second reason that this was such a monumental moment is because this would be the first time, we would share our story in detail. I say "our" and "we" because this is not just my story—but my mom's story, as well. I spoke to my extended family to gather their thoughts on if I should proceed. To my surprise, there was little, if any, reluctance. One of my cousins texted me later that week and said, "Go for it!"

The op-ed titled, *Me, My Mom and Schizophrenia* became the second most publicly vulnerable experience I had to date. For my mom, it was even more revealing. For the first time, we were speaking to an innumerable audience about a personal experience that, to be quite honest, I was more comfortable with hiding. However, I knew that it was time to own our truth and lend a voice to the countless others who had been silenced by fear, stigma and *schizophrenia.*

It baffles me that thirteen letters had the power to inflict so much pain and stigma. Though our thirteen letters spelled *schizophrenia,* for many others, the thirteen letters *mental illness* carry the same shame. Schizophrenia is a mental disorder characterized by abnormal thinking, perceptual disturbances, and diminished or exaggerated emotional expression ("Schizophrenia - Symptoms and causes," 2020). For as long as I can remember, my mother has struggled with this mental health disorder. According to records I have seen, and conversations with family and friends, mom began showing symptoms in her early to mid-twenties. She was finally diagnosed with *schizophrenia* in her late 20s. Though several relatives report her having lengthy periods of lucidness, in spite of those accounts, to my knowledge, my mom has not been able to lead an independent life for more than thirty years. The presence of mental illness created many challenges for our family, especially for us—her children.

2 | FRIED EGGS AND BACON

The smell of bacon and eggs filled my nostrils and drew me from my slumber. When I reached the kitchen, there stood my mom at the black and white stove, dodging the popping grease. The stench of old grease stored in the family-size Folgers® coffee can sometimes became unbearable at breakfast. Somehow, I stomached through it because it was an opportunity to be around my mom. She did not cook often. But when she did, it was usually breakfast. After sitting me at the large table with the pink cushioned chairs, she plated my food. She jellied the butter toasted Wonder Bread® and scooped out a hefty portion of scrambled eggs made from the powder mix. She placed the white plate with blue and pink flowers before me and turned back to the stove. She grabbed a few pieces of bacon and gently laid them on the plate before darting out of the kitchen to the next room.

Not long after mom made her exit, the chocolate brown door that separated our apartment from the next opened.

My grandmother's voice rang out, "Tony, it's time for you to get dressed."

Living with a parent who has a mental health disorder was quite the struggle. According to new research, "children living with parents with severe mental illness encounter specific stressors related to disrupted life routines, repeated episodes of illness and hospitalization of their parents, causing fracturing of family, academic and social lives." ("Defining Quality of Life in the Children of Parents With Severe Mental Illness: A Preliminary Stakeholder-Led Model," 2013)

It has been long stated that children of parents with mental illness have an increased risk of developing mental disorders themselves. But the impact of parental mental illness does not end there. Children of patients with schizophrenia exhibited poorer school performance in comparison to children of parents with no diagnosis ("Poor school performance in offspring of patients with schizophrenia: What are the mechanisms?" 2012).

Perhaps someone had enlightened my grandmother on the stats. It was like she knew that if she did not provide oversight, my siblings and I would never make it to school on time. So, every day, this was our routine—at least when mom was not in the local psychiatric hospital.

One of the main contributors to poor school performance for children with parents who have mental illness is the existence of *toxic stress* in our homes. Mental illness in homes can be linked to reduced family functioning. It is believed, or *so I have been told* that the family is a child's first and core arena of development. It is within the family that a child attains his or her language, character, social and emotional aptitude (Allen, 2015). In homes where parental mental illness exists, children are often subjected to family conflict, violence and other negative life events that can severely impair their growth and development.

As a survivor, I can tell you firsthand of the challenges we faced—and the residual effects in my life today. The smell of fried eggs and bacon teleports me back to those early mornings in the kitchen. I vividly, and admittedly, often recollect on those mornings in the kitchen with my mom.

Even with my daughter, I laugh when she asks, "Daddy, what is your favorite meal?"

Emphatically, I reply, "Breakfast, of course."

3 | THE PUSH

Watching my daughter grow up and encounter the world is perhaps the reason why I thought telling our story is imperative. She has seen firsthand my mother's outbursts and, as she grew older, she inquired about them. But just as I felt in the writing of the op-ed, I remain free. I know this goes against most schools of thought, but I needed to write the op-ed and now this book—selfishly, for me. The experience is freeing and life-giving. Finally, I am able to give voice to my experience. But, more importantly, I learned there were so many others facing the same set of challenges.

When the op-ed went public, almost immediately, the comments and reviews began pouring into my inbox. Complete strangers from around the United States and the world read our story. Perhaps more importantly, they were able to identify with it. I shared a few of the messages with my mom. She was touched and, every so often, she asked me about the article. As the years have gone by, we continue to receive notes via email and social media of appreciation for sharing our story. Each message served as a reminder of the numerous lives that have been impacted directly or indirectly by mental illness.

Several of the notes stuck with me. But one note in particular read:

> "For so many years, I felt like no one could understand the tremendous weight of being the child of a parent with mental illness. Then came your article. Thank you!"

Another one read:

> "My mom had been undiagnosed for fifteen years until this past January (2016). The timeliness of your article has freed me from the guilt I have felt in being her caregiver."

However, one of the most memorable messages came into my inbox on May 18, 2016. The message read:

> "Good morning Mr. Jackson,
>
> Thank you for writing and sharing your story in *Me, My Mom and Schizophrenia*. I really cannot express my sincere gratitude for your story. I know you are a

busy man, so I do not want to take up too much of your time, but please know your story is so very powerful!

My oldest sister lives with Bipolar Disorder and, like your mother, it has been very challenging for her to be able to take care of her son (my nephew) while also taking care of herself and the challenges of living with a mental illness. At various points in the past, my nephew has lived/stayed with other family members. But three years ago, my sister and I decided it would be best for my nephew to live with me permanently. I have to admit - I was not always the most supportive person to my sister and the illness that shook our world. I didn't understand mental illness, and my lack of understanding was a huge roadblock to having compassion for my sister. When my sister and me came to this decision, I knew I had to educate myself and challenge my perceptions in order to provide as much support, care and love to [my nephew]. He had to see my genuine love and compassion for his mom. We are in such a different place today. But this experience has really made me understand how few (if any) resources there are out there for children and families in this situation. I know because I have searched and searched! I can't express to you the heartache it causes me when, to this day, I have other family members who are so quick to praise me, but so quick to say how they, "…don't understand how a mom can give her child up like she did" instead of seeing how remarkable this was for my sister to make this decision because she absolutely loves [her son]. There is no book out there to guide us in our journey. We struggle and we prevail. But more than anything, we love. My sister and my relationship today, is the best that it has ever been (though there is always room for growth) and [my nephew] is doing so, so well.

Thank you for taking the time to read this and thank you for sharing."

The writer of this note epitomized the audience to whom we hoped to reach in sharing our story. Her transparent recounting of the emotions and feelings about mental health became the impetus for this literary work. Her words were piercing: "…this experience has really made me understand how few (if any) resources there are out there for children and families in this situation." My prayer is that this book serves as a resource for families who find themselves in this situation—a tool to spur conversation.

4 | NOVEMBER 1951

The year 1951 brought with it a number of commemorative moments to the world. Major League Baseball catcher for the Brooklyn Dodgers, Roy Campanella, won the first of his three National League MVP Awards. The British auto manufacturers Austin and Morris Motors merged. The United States performed nuclear tests at the Nevada Test Site, and the first rocket to intercept an airplane happened in White Sands, New Mexico. But November 1951 proved to be a grand moment for a family in the clay hills of Mississippi as a young girl made her way into the world.

On what the almanac would call a fairly warm day in November of that year, a young woman named Marie gave birth to fraternal twins. One of them was my mother. Mom's birth marks the beginning of our story right there in Holmes County, Mississippi. A small community then and now, today boasting a population of about 20,000 residents, Holmes County is bordered on the west by the Yazoo River and the east by the Big Black River. The first of a dizygotic birth—the medical term for fraternal twins—my mom went on to be raised in a small town known as *Tchula*. This funny-named town was in western Holmes County, located along the Tchula River in the Delta of Mississippi. If oral family history serves me correctly, my mom was the third oldest of nine children born to my maternal grandmother.

Today, Holmes County is said to be a "great place to call home" with its small community charm and southern hospitality. However, Tchula remains small and is currently experiencing economic, health and social challenges. The major industry is farming; however, poor education and limited financial resources have made those owners sell and/or rent their land.

The county seat is in Lexington, Mississippi, which was named in honor of Lexington, Massachusetts. The county is named after David Holmes, the first governor of the state of Mississippi who later became United States Senator for Mississippi. These details became relevant to me as I listened to my mother's monologue during any one of her schizophrenic hallucinations.

Though she was born free (not a slave), my mother's birth came just as the Civil Rights Movement was beginning in the early 1950s. Jim Crow Laws—any law that enforced racial segregation in the South—were still in effect in many of the communities where she lived. Cotton had long been the commodity crop, and prior to the Civil War, slave labor was used to cultivate the cotton fields owned by white planters. Following the Civil War, many freed slaves acquired land under the New Deal in the Delta by clearing and selling timber. By the 1960s, it is believed that over fifty percent of the land was owned by African Americans. As the Civil Rights Movement took shape, a large majority of those African Americans lost ownership during the harsh financial times—going on or returning to sharecropping to survive.

The expanding modernization of farm labor, the creation of defense industry jobs in the west, and continued African American migration caused Holmes County to see significant population declines between 1940 and 1970. The abrupt migration caused the significantly agriculture-based economy to suffer. The great migration from the south to the west and northern states found my family, as well. In as early as 1961, the first members of my family began moving north.

Some settled in Wisconsin and Illinois, while the vast majority of my mom's siblings settled in Detroit, Michigan.

According to oral history, my mom arrived in Detroit the first time in the early 60s. She remained in Detroit for a few months, but later returned to Mississippi. There she gave birth to my eldest brother, Steven. After his birth, my mom returned to Detroit, where she lived with her sister. While in Detroit, Steven died of Sudden Infant Death Syndrome (SIDS)—the unexplained death, usually during sleep, of a seemingly healthy baby less than a year old. Though not certain, this is believed to have been the stimulus to her mental break. According to Mayo Clinic, the exact cause of schizophrenia is not known, but a combination of genetics, environment, and altered brain chemistry and structure may play a role ("Schizophrenia - Symptoms and causes," 2020). Following Steven's death, my mom left Detroit again for the south—perhaps seeking a change in scenery. Who could blame her after the untimely death of her infant son?

After a few years, my mom returned to Detroit in the mid-70s but, this time, with two small children in tow. Perhaps to the surprise of many, while away in Mississippi, my mom met a man and conceived two children with him: my brother Jeffrey and sister Kyra. Upon arriving in Detroit, she went again to live with her sister. She did return to

Mississippi for short visits over the years, but Detroit ultimately became her home.

5 | NEW CITY, NEW CHALLENGES AND NEW BIRTH

Mom's transition to Detroit was met with all things new. She found refuge with her oldest sister, my maternal aunt. In interviewing my aunt for this book, she described how my mom was a tremendous babysitter, caring for her children (my mom's nephew and niece) while she (my aunt) worked two jobs. There is limited knowledge of my mother ever holding a job or being gainfully employed. During this time, my mom was said to be in stable mental condition—though she had moments of perceptual disturbances. The family saw it only as residue of her infant son's death.

A lover of music, and one who enjoys it with all of her being, Mom would often be heard playing classics like "I've Been Lonely for So Long" by Frederick Knight or "Why Have I Lost You" by Cameo. A quick listen to the songs makes me think my mom saw her fair share of heartbreak and found solace in the music. Mental illness is neither necessary nor sufficient for an appreciation of the arts. However, "moderate- to low-quality evidence suggests that music therapy as an addition to standard care improves the global state, mental state (including negative and general symptoms), social functioning, and quality of life of people with schizophrenia or schizophrenia-like disorders." (Music therapy for people with schizophrenia and schizophrenia-like disorders, 2017)

Mom continued living with her sister until she later moved into an apartment of a three-family unit. Located on what was then known as the west side of the city of Detroit, the three-family unit seemed to be just what the doctor had ordered for the close-knit family. The other two apartments were occupied by her mother (my maternal grandmother) and another sister (my maternal aunt). Family accounts say it was during my mother's time at that home when they began to see significant declines in her mental health. Fits of rage, anger and violence—though short lived—were the norm. As the years went by, my mother's mental health continued down a slippery slope.

After some time, my grandmother had to petition Mom into the local psychiatric hospital. This became a repeat occurrence. By the early 80s, her diagnosis was documented as schizophrenia. My grandmother, I'm sure supported by my aunts, worked tirelessly to secure Social Security disability benefits for my mother to lessen the economic blow to the family. The inability to maintain a job, let alone carry out the day to day functions of home management and childrearing, created a rather dismal situation. Coupled with the absence of a husband, the family outlook was bleak. Families with parental mental illness are less likely to see positive financial outcomes. The unemployment rate of individuals with mental illness, especially amongst minorities, is significantly higher than those without mental illness. Thus, the financial burden a family faces can be a heavy load to bear.

During all of this transition, an additional weight was placed on an already fragile family. My now eldest living brother, Jeffrey, was about five or six years old when he took a fall from a window of the upper level apartment where he resided with my mother and sister. The fall caused some physical damage to his body, but significant brain impairment. I am told he had to undergo several rounds of surgery and rehabilitation. Over the next few years, the family was forced to deal with a new normal. That experience only added weight to my mother's already fragile mental state. In the years following, my mom did all she could to care for my brother and sister with significant help from my maternal aunts and grandmother.

As the years progressed, the weight of caring for an adult child with a mental health disorder, with two children and one who is developmentally incapacitated, took a toll on my grandmother. She suffered a nervous breakdown (or mental breakdown: a period of intense mental stress). Thankfully, she rebounded! She soon took charge of my mother's care and that of my siblings. Over the course of time, there were periods of sustained stability; however, when things broke down, the impact was tough. By the mid-80s, my grandmother and my mom's siblings had become used to managing the perceptual disturbances.

Then came the spring of 1985.

6 | SPRING 1985

The year 1985 in Detroit was no flowery bed of ease for residents. According to an article published in *The Chicago Tribune*, the city had 636 murders in 1985. At that time, it was the highest murder rate of the nation's largest cities, a rate more than twice that of Chicago. It was a record year of homicides in the city. By the end of the next year, the number of murders had soared to ten more than the previous year, which included the deaths of forty-three children under the age of sixteen (Franklin, 1987). Subsequently, the city's population experienced a steady decline. Yet, on a spring Sunday afternoon in May of 1985, I found my way through the birth canals of a mother with schizophrenia. Like so many of the children born at that time, Mom delivered at the local Hutzel Women's Hospital.

According to my aunts, my mom had become involved with a man. Obvious, I know. But the details of who he is, when they met and where she met him all remain to be known. However, family accounts say her pregnancy with me was one of those times of sustained lucidness. She did not appear to be in any mental distress, discomfort, diminished or exaggerated emotional expression. In fact, one aunt said, "Your mother was known for cracking jokes. She would more often than not be causing a stir with her laughter." This same aunt told me, an account consistent with that of my late grandmother (1926 -2009), that the date of my birth was a pretty calm experience.

On the second Sunday of May 1985, Mother's Day, my mother gave birth to yours truly. At just about the time when everyone would have been on the way to church, my mom's water broke at the house. She was transported by taxi cab to the hospital, accompanied by her youngest and second oldest sisters. I am told that delivery was fairly easy and no major complications followed. After giving birth, my mom is said to have held me and took pleasure in naming me Antoine DeJuan Jackson. I later learned that the name Antoine was suggested by her niece, whom she had cared for while living with her eldest sister. I must admit, for a long while, I assumed someone saw the street sign "Saint

Antoine" where the hospital was located and decided to name me after it. Hey, you can't blame a guy for trying.

The naming of a child is huge in black culture. I remember growing up hearing various accounts of who was responsible for naming children in the family. So, to whomever deserves the credit, I say, "Thank you!" for naming me! Antoine is a pretty dope name, and it was my grandmother who taught me its meaning. Perhaps she had taken a glimpse into the future and could see my need for encouragement. So, she let me know early that my name meant "highly praiseworthy" or "deserving of approval and admiration." After all, growing up in a home with mental illness left me many days feeling like I had been dealt a bad hand of UNO cards!

7 | GROWING UP IN MENTAL ILLNESS

On what is now considered the southwest side of Detroit, my mother, brother, sister and I lived. The first house I remember us living in was that three-family unit apartment. It was a bike ride or intense walking distance from the famous Tiger Stadium. Not the best of neighborhoods, but we had neighbors. There was the community auto mechanic who worked on vehicles in his yard. The local resale stores. These became my favorite places to visit as I grew older. A plethora of small businesses that sold clothes, jewelry and other fashion items, and the local party store. Each of these places were important landmarks in my childhood.

Some of my earliest memories include my mother taking me to preschool and kindergarten at Newberry Elementary, which is now torn down. Those were the days when neighborhood children only needed to walk a few blocks to attend school. So much of that has changed in the city. School was a hard adjustment for me. I can remember crying for my mom to not leave me or to come back as I saw her walk away from the building through the large plexiglass windows of the breezeway that connected the new building to the old structure. She never turned around to save me from Ms. Green's preschool or Ms. Dupree's kindergarten class.

Our walks to school had a recurring soundtrack. My mom talked to herself, usually uttering obscenities and a storyline fit for the best action flick you could ever find. The older I got, the more embarrassed I became of her—especially when I noticed other parents and children keeping a "healthy distance" from us. Some were more obvious than others, but I watched closely as they sped up walking or crossed to the opposite side of the street.

Though embarrassing at times, the walks to school with my mom were fun. Probably, because unlike my grandmother, mom would let me walk free of holding her hand. Admittedly, I did not mind as much because I could play it off when she got too loud, verbalizing her mental hallucinations.

Though what I am describing happened over 25 years ago, there remains this same experience for children all around the word. Children being raised in a home with mental illness is not uncommon today. "Worldwide, an estimated one in five children, ages 0-17 years old, has a parent with mental illness. These children are at higher risk of developing a mental illness themselves" ("Identification of Children of Parents With Mental Illness: A Necessity to Provide Relevant Support," 2020). This is quite possibly the greatest trauma of being the child of a parent with mental illness—worrying if, or when, it will happen to you.

As I recollect, my heart is fixed to believe that my mom did her best to care for us—with support and help from my grandmother and aunts. Growing up, I knew something was different about my family. But I could never find the words to string together an articulate sentence. As an adult now, I call to mind how our home was—dare I say—a calm incubator the first through the eighth of each month. However, after that, it became one of the most toxic places to live for a child.

According to The Center on the Developing Child at Harvard University, "The future of any society depends on its ability to foster the healthy development of the next generation. Research on the biology of stress demonstrates that healthy development can be derailed by excessive or prolonged activation of stress response systems in the body and brain. Such toxic stress can have damaging effects on learning, behavior, and health across the lifespan" (Harvard University, 2019).

The idea of toxic stress had not reached its prevalence back then as it has today. Nonetheless, though nameless or not clearly defined, the impacts were felt. "Toxic stress response can occur when a child experiences strong, frequent, and/or prolonged adversity—such as physical or emotional abuse, chronic neglect, caregiver substance abuse or mental illness, exposure to violence, and/or the accumulated burdens of family economic hardship—without adequate adult support. This kind of prolonged activation of the stress response systems can disrupt the development of brain architecture and other organ systems, and increase the risk for stress-related disease and cognitive impairment, well into the adult years (Harvard University, 2019).

8 | THE FIRST THROUGH THE EIGHTH

The seemingly sudden changes to our home atmosphere sent me into a tailspin of emotions. By the eighth day of each month, the monies my mom had received in the form of Supplemental Security Income (SSI) for both her and my brother, including food stamps, had run out. Supplemental Security Income (SSI) is a program managed by the Social Security Administration, but SSI is not paid for by Social Security taxes. The United States Treasury general funds pay for SSI. These monthly payments are made to people who have low income and few resources, and who are 65 or older; blind; or disabled ("Supplemental Security Income," 2020). With my mom's diagnosis, and my brother's disability, our family was a two-time recipient. Not to mention, my mother received welfare benefits from the state for us that included food stamps.

What was for certain is that, by the eighth day of each month, chaos was the order of the day. I'm not sure if any bills were paid, but I knew the money was gone. Typically, the checks came on the first of each month in a light blue envelope. My mom stood watch, looking for the mail carrier. If by chance they were late (any time past the normal period she had calculated), she'd willingly take a trip through the neighborhood, looking for them. I remember taking a few of those trips with her.

Once she got the checks in hand, we'd gather and head to the local party story, where my mom cashed the checks. Mike, presumably the store owner, was a Chaldean, "Mr. Debonair" type guy who stood about six feet tall. He knew my mom by name and went out of his way to make sure she was taken care of. I stood by watching as my mom signed the back of the checks, inked her thumb, and pressed it on the back of the checks in the square box. After presenting the check with her state identification card to Mike, he counted out to her the monies. As I grew older, I came to understand that the money he counted out to her was less the check cashing fee—including payoff for any balance my mom had accrued in the weeks prior. This amount ranged anywhere from $50 to $100.

She'd allow us to go get a few snacks—typically some sugary drinks, cookies, chips and candy. We then crossed the busy thoroughfare and went to the shop owned by the Chinese-American couple. Depending on the time of year, we'd all get a new outfit to wear. We then moved down to what I simply knew as the "Food Stamp Office" where Mom got food stamps. As I got older, she ripped out and gave each of us a few dollars from the brown booklet. Sometimes we got a few from the green booklet. From there, we went over to the grocery store, where she would load the basket with food, paying for it with the food stamps. Then, we caught a ride from a jitney back to the house. We'd live out the next eight or so days in a calm incubator. Though the process of check cashing and shopping was wide-ranging each month, it was usually with the same level of energy.

Research has shown that in families with parental psychiatric diagnoses, family functioning was worse in comparison to families with no occurrences of psychiatric diagnoses. Poor family functioning is observed in cohesion, adaptability, organization and the quality of communication within a family ("Family Functioning and Psychological Health of Children with Mentally Ill Parents," 2019). More often than not, the challenges of mental illness are seen in the extended family members, especially children.

54

9 | SHE'S NOT CRAZY, JUST SICK

For a long time, I was not able to fully understand my mother's condition. But who expected me to understand? Honestly, *I did*. I had taken on a responsibility that was too big for me. This is not uncommon of a child with a parent with mental illness. I expected myself to know and understand what was wrong with my mom. By the time I reached first grade, it seemed like most of the kids in my class knew me as "the boy with the crazy momma." A few were bold enough—or perhaps just showing their age—to verbalize it to me. Embarrassed and irritated, I would fire back flippantly, "She's not crazy! Just sick!" After all, that was the narrative I had been hearing since I could remember. Sometimes it was said in a loving, affirming way. Other times, it seemed to be a dart thrown right at my heart. Nevertheless, I wanted to get a better understanding. But from whom? Surely not my mom, right? I couldn't go to her and ask, "What is wrong with you?" The answer probably would have been, "Nothing" or circumstantial to that present moment. I certainly did not believe she would be able to articulate to me in such a way that I could build a narrative to share with others when they inquired of me.

But, that would all soon change.

School soon became a problem for me. Chronic absenteeism set in motion a chain of unpleasant experiences. Perhaps through no fault of my own, I missed a large number of days. If my memory serves me well, I was in second grade when the truancy officer came to our home. I remember the knock at the door as I sat watching television in my grandmother's bed. I knew the voice, but I didn't understand why she had come to the house. She asked for my mom. My grandmother, presumably aware of the reason for the visit, seemed to ignore her request. She inquired how she could help.

"Antoine has been absent and tardy for a majority of the semester, and we're required to do a home visit."

I became scared to my core. I ran through the door that separated my grandmother's apartment from the one I shared with my mom, brother and sister. Mom was in the bed sleeping. I darted back through the door and saw my grandmother closing the door that led downstairs to the front entry door. She told me to go back and sit down to watch television.

Granny called for my mom through the chocolate brown door to come into the room. When she came in, she said, "That school came looking for this boy because he missing too many days."

My mom seemingly unphased, wiping sleep from her eyes, replied, "I'll take him tomorrow," and left the room. Though I cannot remember all the happenings from that moment to the next, I vividly recall how, over time, much of my belongings were moved into my grandmother's apartment and the increased amount of time I spent there.

I later learned that my grandmother had agreed to take me in to ensure that I got to school to prohibit the school from contacting child protective services.

10 | MY SAVING GRACE, MARIE

Living with my grandmother was cool. I got first dibs on all her baked goods—many times being able to lick the bowl of the remaining cake or sweet potato pie batter. However, living with my grandmother meant seeing my mom from a different angle. As I got older, I noticed how managing the mental illness became increasingly a challenge for our family. Her insistence that people were stealing her money, or that someone was in her apartment, became regular occurrences. The abnormal thinking and perceptual disturbances seemed to be regular. They usually happened at or near the first of each month. The warmer months brought on public displays of anger and aggression.

One day, my mom was out front of the house yelling and screaming at my aunts and grandmother, all of whom were trying to settle her down. She insisted that they had stolen her check from the mail. We later discovered the check had been mistakenly delivered to the wrong house by the mail carrier. Unfortunately, while all the chaos was happening, the neighbor was still at work and had not retrieved his mail to discover the discrepancy. No one could stop my mom that day. She had created a narrative in her mind and was willing to physically harm anyone who came against it and her.

My aunt loved to garden and had prepared a nice flower bed in front of the three-family unit. It sat between the two staircases that led to the long-shared porch. In the garden were bricks my aunt had taken and painted white to give accent to the garden. In hindsight, her efforts made for nice curb appeal. That day, my mom was in a fit of rage. She had been known in times past to brandish knives at the family. But, on this day, she grabbed a brick. By the time I came downstairs to see what all the commotion was about, my mom had thrown one of the white painted bricks through the windows along the front porch that led to my aunt's apartment.

The window instantly shattered and the panic of the moment was crazy. My grandmother had already called the police. By this time, they were on the scene. My mom retreated to the house and got a knife. She was now wielding it at the officers, my aunts and grandmother. I distinctly remember the female police officer (who some twenty years later I would meet) taking me off to the side. I didn't realize until after what she was doing. She did not want me to see the two male officers as they had to physically restrain my mother to the ground. She was transported in handcuffs to the local psychiatric hospital facility.

I wish I could say this was the only occurrence to this magnitude. Sadly, it was not.

Before long, my mom had been to the psychiatric hospital so much that I looked forward to visiting her there. The one hospital had the huge fish tank with all the colorful fish—I liked to visit that one. What I liked more was that, when I accompanied my grandmother and aunts to see my mom, she seemed happier. Her smile was bright and radiant. Most times, she was wearing earrings! Internally, I had determined that whenever mom was wearing earrings, she was feeling better. She typically only wore earrings around the first of the month when finances came in, or when she had an important appointment to attend. Needless to say, I wished she had worn earrings more.

What I did not prepare for was the day I would get an understanding of what my mom was living through. But that day finally arrived. It happened rather organically. My grandmother had long been a client of the local insurance firm, and the agent came by the house to collect the premiums. He was a rather tall white guy, who sat with his legs crossed and drank my grandmother's coffee.

She would often confide in me after he left, "I'm glad he ain't ask for no more of my coffee."

Coffee became the least of my worries following one of his monthly visits. On one particular occasion, he and my grandmother were discussing insurance policies for all of us—my mother, brother, sister and me. Perhaps worried that things might go south, or just being the wise woman she was, she wanted to have something in place for us. I vividly remember them engaging in a pretty lengthy conversation. My grandmother repeatedly reminded him that she was on a fixed income herself. At one point in the conversation, he did his all too familiar, "Believe me Mrs. Rosco, I understand." Finally, sitting his coffee mug on the table, he looked at my grandmother and said, "The insurance policy will be quite expensive for her ... because of her schizophrenia."

Their conversation came long before I had heard anyone else use the term referring to my mom. Besides being too young to remember it, this was my first time hearing the word used to describe my mother's condition. Even more, we lived in a predominantly black, inner-city community and attended a classical Pentecostal church. In those circles, you were either crazy or demon-possessed.

11 | MENTAL ILLNESS IN THE BLACK COMMUNITY AND BLACK CHURCHES

Within the historical context, the African American (or black) community has endured numerous episodes and events of abuse, discrimination and intimidation. These experiences have profoundly impacted our mental health, resulting in increased instances of anxiety, stigmatization and depression. Much of the mental health crisis facing the black community can be traced back to the atrocities of slavery, periods of sustained racial bias, and adversities in sharecropping. There has been a long history of trauma in the black community. Even still, we see how racial exclusion from education, health, social and economic resources further impaired us as a people.

Despite the best efforts, the historical instances of our past continue to reverberate in our present day. The

Black community still faces high unemployment rates, low educational attainment, and lower financial status in comparison to our Caucasian counterparts. Additional challenges, such as poverty, substance abuse problems and homelessness, pile on to an already precipitous situation. Many of these factors have direct correlation with mental health issues in our communities. Despite the previous efforts of advocacy and inclusion to equal national rights, attitudes of rejection continue to occur, causing many to seek out religious and spiritual intervention. But are our religious communities and organizations prepared to confront such an issue as mental health?

Changing the Approach, the Church is Taking to Address Mental Health

Including the religious and church community in the management of mental health issues is critical to our success as a people. As one of the key elements in the life of most black people, the church can serve as a key player in mental health promotion activities. Although churches aim to present and nurture relationship with God, they have the great opportunity to encourage families and mental health patients to seek out, utilize and continue mental health treatments.

Notably, one of the main challenges in addressing the psychological problems of the community members is the aspect of compliance with healthcare procedures. A large percentage of the mental health issues in black patients is related to substance abuse, which can first be managed through setting the right attitudes and perspective toward the need for intervention. Churches play the crucial role of influencing a person's behavior into the proper conduct of life and ethical standards. The communication functions, community cohesion and sustainability initiatives highly depend on collaboration between a faith-based entity and a healthcare profession that, in return, would facilitate the recovery of mental health patients.

As churches are changing their approach, success is being observed in organizations where several key elements are in play. Organizations that are training and educating the clergy about the clear signs and symptoms of psychological issues are seeing an increase in self-reporting and utilization of mental health services. Furthermore, as churches begin the promotion of mental health treatment options among the black communities, and work to reduce the stigma linked with mental illness, change is happening. But the church by itself cannot do it. As the healthcare industry continues to evolve, successful intervention is also related to a broad approach of patient-centered care, which involves engaging the patient in the management of mental health issues.

Improvement Initiative for Churches in Addressing Mental Health Issues

One of the ways in which the faith-based community can further reduce mental health issues in black patients is by reducing its furtherance of stigmatization. Instead, church leaders should adopt a willingness to fully concentrate on listening to the needs of the individuals. The church is at the forefront of influencing societal ethical standards and, in most cases, it participates in condemning acts of evil and unacceptable standards at the community levels. The church should continue this route, but it should focus some of its time and resources to work with community mental health agencies to families and individuals burdened by mental illness. The idea is not for the church to have all the answers; the goal is to help support the work of mental health professionals and organizations by fighting against the stigma.

In my travels, I was blessed to visit several faith communities in the United States who were unabashedly tackling mental illness. One ministry developed a "get-help" line where families can reach out for counseling when going through mental health, substance abuse, gambling or . domestic issues. This is one example of the church's response in black communities to effectively manage mental illness.

I am personally thankful to see the progress the church has made in the conversations around mental illness. As mentioned, I have witnessed several faith-based organizations take on leading roles to address mental illness within their local congregations and communities. And, while I could personally ascribe these developments to a few leading personalities, perhaps the greatest change agents have been the brave men and women who decided to speak up and out about mental illness.

12 | FAITH AT THE CENTER

For as long as I can remember, my family has attended church. Some more than others, but there has always been some level of participation. This bit of information does not necessarily make us an anomaly either. Especially when you consider that African-Americans have higher reported rates of church attendance and religiosity than other ethnic groups.

In retrospect, as a child, church attendance became an outlet from the sometimes-chaotic enterprise known as home. I had watched for some years from afar as my aunt, her children and grandchildren attended church. Though my immediate family had gone on occasion, we certainly didn't have the same devotion, in my opinion, as them. We were more "CME" members. You know, the ones who attend church on Christmas, Mother's Day and Easter. My aunt's family was more involved. I recall how members of the church came by during funerals and prayed for our family—all because my aunt was a member of the church. *How cool!* I thought.

As I grew older, I embraced religion. My first encounters were with my grandmother, who would rehearse the Scriptures in my hearing, and my aunt, who I would hear praying downstairs in the lower apartment. At the time, I thought she had gone mad—speaking in some gibberish. I later learned that she was speaking in tongues—an ability given to believers by God. All of this stuff was becoming more and more interesting to me. My palette had become whet with excitement to learn and experience more.

Soon, I stopped referring to it as "embracing religion" and instead gladly told people I was embracing my *faith*. By the time I had reached fourth grade, my mind was set that, one day, I would be a preacher. After all, the gospel of Jesus Christ is one of the greatest stories of overcoming obstacles known to man. My grandmother often reminded me that a good preacher must be able to read, so doing homework was a must.

Her reminder bolstered my commitment to school. I excelled in my grades and my behavior gradually changed. Though, despite the good behavior at school and church, I was a hypocrite at home. Easily offended, I was impatient with others. I internalized their disdain as being targeted at my mother and her children. As a result, I often lashed out in cursing rants. I thought I was defending my family. Repeatedly angered by, what I thought, were insensitive comments, I found myself getting into trouble often.

The older I became, thank God for grace and my grandmother Marie, my anger subsided—or I simply learned how to manage it. My grandmother had to remind me that my soul was in jeopardy of hell fire, unless I learned to forgive those who angered me. She rehearsed in my hearing Mark 8:36-37, *For what shall it profit a man, if he shall gain the whole world, and lose his own soul? Or what shall a man give in exchange for his soul?* Seemingly capitalizing on the moment, she would remind me that the commandment to "honor thy father and mother was nonnegotiable." Despite my mother's mental status, God still intended for me to honor my mother. Her incessant reminders still ring in the hallways of my mind today—and I share them with my daughter.

My faith was taking center stage and soon, everything I did seemed to be connected to it. As I grew in my faith, a peace about my life seemed to follow. However, for every win there seemed to be double the amount of losses. Committed to making myself into a productive contributor of society, my grandmother did her utmost best to keep before me God, both in her prayers and physically by sending me to church. She often told me that the Bible was God's personal love letter to me, and whenever I needed a reminder to go read it.

13 | BAPTIZED INTO IT

Though she never held the title, my grandmother was a missionary evangelist par excellence. She often spent her Saturday mornings making a large breakfast for everyone in the house. Following the meal, she would spend up to three hours sharing nuggets of wisdom with those gathered. One of her favorites was reciting Matthew 6:33 to us: *But seek ye first the kingdom of God and His righteousness and all these things shall be added unto you* (King James Version Bible). She admittedly told us of her failed attempts in life, but reminded us constantly of God's hand of grace and mercy to her. Soon, her voice became embedded in me like a soundtrack. In those occasions when I wanted to do wrong, I could hear her voice ringing out. Even today, sometimes I find myself rehearsing some of her talks to my daughter and youth from around the nation during speaking engagements. She implanted words in me that yielded the greatest harvest we could ever hope for in a person—*change.*

To me, it seemed like a long time, but I can remember how my good behavior and actions in class caught the attention of a few classmates and teachers. They started calling me "Preacher man," or "Preacher Poley," the sketch comedy character from the pop-culture classic, "In Living Color." I did not care for the title as much because, within me, I still struggled to behave accordingly. I really desired to be true to my faith. I did not want to be a hypocrite. That was a word my mom had talked about before. And the description she gave made me not ever want to be one.

One day while playing with my cousins, my aunt was, as she had from time to time, hosting Bible study at her home. It was nice to see the group of women sitting around the table discussing Scriptures. On occasion, one of the brothers from the church would stop by, but I cannot recall their regular attendance in the sessions. I vividly remember these gatherings because I was seemingly drawn into the house just so I could get a glimpse or hear a portion of their discussion. When I became an adult, my aunt and her friends told me that I would occasionally stand around the doorway that led to the room they were in, listening as they discussed the Scriptures. This was true to my memory because I was in search of answers.

By age nine, I had made up my mind that I wanted more of this church and God thing. Whatever it was, I believed it to be better than what I had already. I remember asking my grandmother if I could start taking the church bus with my aunt to church. She obliged! However, whenever I got into some trouble—no matter the magnitude—I noticed my grandmother would threaten to prohibit me from church. Perhaps she had observed my keen interest in church. As time went along, my mom, brother and sister came to church on occasion, usually on Christmas, Mother's Day and Easter. I told you we were a "CME" family.

After a few years, now a pre-teen, I remember telling my grandmother that I wanted to be saved. That was church lingo for wanting to accept Jesus as my personal savior and being baptized. She asked me a series of questions and explained that I had reached the age of accountability, which was twelve years old. As such, my commitment to the faith had to be certain and I could not waiver. My heart was set and my mind had been made up.

It was Mother's Day 1997. Our pastor had just finished his sermon. Like every Sunday before, he began his altar appeal. Usually that was my cue to become distracted.

As he made the altar appeal, I rejected my usual playing with my socks and headed down the center aisle to the front. The blue carpet seemed to never end. Before long, I was standing in front of one of the altar workers.

She asked, "Do you want to be saved?"

I replied with a nod and she insisted I speak audibly. Before long, I was changed out of my houndstooth gray and black suit for all white pants, a t-shirt, socks and a choir robe that was clearly too big. I got baptized and the moment was refreshing. I had no idea it would be the start of the next chapter of life for me—*for us*.

14 | THE AGE OF ACCOUNTABILITY

Sunday, May 11, 1997 was the day before my twelfth birthday. This was my golden birthday—the year you turn the same age as your birthdate. I was turning twelve on the twelfth. It was an exciting time. I would soon be a teenager. Now, some of the things I had longed to do, I would be able to do. Things like riding my bike around the neighborhood and not just on the block. I was free to ride the bus alone and, more importantly, my granny approved me to talk on the phone with a girl. For my grandmother, turning twelve had greater semblance and importance. I remember her telling me that Sunday evening as we prepared for bed, "Tony, you've reached the age of accountability now. You got to be serious and mean Jesus."

This was nothing new to me. For years I had been told about "the age of accountability." But what was it? The notion of an age of accountability is that there is a certain age at which people become accountable to respond to the gospel of Jesus. Before this time, many believed that a child's sins were laid upon his or her parents because they were not old enough to understand. Though there are differing schools of thought, the age of twelve and thirteen have been recognized as "the ages of accountability." Whatever it was, I certainly wanted none of it. For me, the age of accountability simply meant that I had more responsibilities as it related to my familial experience.

At eleven years old, I knew how to catch the bus to pay utility bills. When I turned twelve, the responsibilities increased. My grandmother was getting older and the idea of her catching multiple buses was not that suitable, and she did not drive. Soon, my responsibilities around the house increased. This may seem normal for any young twelve-year-old. But the presence of parental mental illness elevates this to an entirely different level.

My grandmother, perhaps for fear of me missing a meal or not being presentable at school, seemed inflexible about teaching me household chores. She was adamant about teaching me how to cook. She would call me in the kitchen and demand that I sit and watch her as she blanched greens, soaked black-eyed peas, or prepared one of her many desserts. Soon after, she moved on to teaching me how to iron clothes, use starch and repair hems with needle and thread. It did not stop there. She would sit by and instruct me to call the credit card companies to process payments, things she did for years on end. Now, I was the person on the phone. It was always funny when the operator on the other end called me Mrs. Rosco because of my pre-puberty voice. When we went to the credit union, my grandmother made sure I was at the window with her. She'd ask the teller to explain the transaction to me. On the way home in the cab or on the bus, she would quiz me on what I was told. Ironically enough, years later, I was employed at a credit union, performing some of those very transactions I had witnessed while accompanying my grandmother.

It is not uncommon for children of parents with mental illness to take on responsibilities to care for parents, siblings and, lastly, themselves. The responsibilities most always exceed our cognitive, emotional and spiritual maturity. As a young caregiver, you may have to take on many of the adult responsibilities associated with parenting and managing a household. Such things might include grocery shopping, budgeting for bills and preparing meals.

On those days when my mom was up to it, she did it well. Whatever she could not do, she had my grandmother and aunts to help with. But the accountability talks continued in my ear. As I grew into my teenage years, I was consistently reminded to, "Get an education because you're going to have to take care of your mom."

Sadly, no one explicitly explained what that *really* meant.

15 | THE MISEDUCATION OF MENTAL ILLNESS

When we consider the vast number of pressures on the lives of children of parents with mental illness, we see an urgent need for a new approach to mental healthcare. Knowing that mental illness affects the entire family, the approach must take into account all members in the home. We need a holistic approach to mental healthcare. Holistic is characterized by the treatment of the whole person, taking into account mental and social factors, rather than just the symptoms of a disease. This is the approach we need applied to mental healthcare in America, especially in minority communities as healthcare disparities and implicit bias linger.

In the context of this book, such an approach means that attention is given to not just the parent patient, but to the child or children in the home. Treating only the parent takes for granted the opportunity to positively affect the child's health and wellness. It is a common belief that children of parents with mental illness are at higher risk of incidents of mental illness themselves. According to the American Academy of Child and Adolescent Psychiatry, "Mental illnesses in parents represent a risk for children in the family. These children have a higher risk for developing mental illnesses than other children" (The American Academy of Child and Adolescent Psychiatry (AACAP), 2015). Mitigating the risks associated with parental mental illness in the lives of children must be a priority of healthcare providers and community social service agencies. The strategies employed must be specific to the black community where, disproportionately, services are limited or not utilized because of stigma.

Growing up in a home where parental mental illness existed, I was plagued by thoughts and realties that were distorted. My mom had narratives that frightened me to my core. Some of her verbal stories included talk of murder, rape, kidnapping and forcible drug use. Oftentimes, her stories left me too unsure of who to trust because some of the characters she mentioned were family and friends. As a child, when I confronted some of the narratives with questions, her answers seemed plausible to my immature mind. However, my grandmother would provide clarity to her stories, often reminding me that my mom was *sick*. I appreciated granny, but I often felt like I did not know who was telling the truth.

The feelings of distrust were growing in the soil of my fears.

I wanted so bad for my mom to be okay! So much so, that I tried to rationalize her irrational behaviors and hallucinations. Every boy wants the love and affection of his mother, and certainly, every child wants to believe their parent tells the truth always. My desire to believe my mom was so strong that I was willing to believe her, even though what she was saying sounded a bit weird. In the years to follow, when I came to understand the disease of schizophrenia, I felt helpless and hopeless. Now the feelings of guilt and shame crept into my mind.

This was the vicious cycle growing up, but this was only the tip of the proverbial iceberg.

16 | QUESTIONS…

Why me? Whose fault is it? Other questions like those often flooded my mind.

Countless times during my adolescent and early adult life, I asked the question, "Why me?" Though I was not the only one in our family facing the challenges of parental mental illness, it felt like it. The questioning usually followed a traumatic uproar or a moment of observing other families. No matter the motivation, the questions, and those that ensued, were the true sentiments of my heart.

Sadly, I did not know how to properly communicate what I was feeling. I had no one who I felt comfortable enough to divulge it to. So, the internal dialogue of self-defeating, self-hating self-talk commenced. Like your favorite track on repeat, the words became second nature to me. Unable to properly place and organize my thoughts, I felt void and reluctant. I know I am not alone in this experience. I have heard countless stories from children of parents with mental illness and their experience with bouts of depression, loneliness and self-defeating, self-talk quite frequently. Asking the questions is our cry for help. And though the questions are not worded the same way each time, the intended outcome is—*a cry for help.*

One day while riding the bus to the mall, I sat on the seat, thinking about the families seated across the row. Immediately, the internal questioning started.

"What did I do to get this life?"

"What about my life, my happiness and my desires?"

"Why can't my family be like theirs?"

My emotions became toxic, and this state of toxicity is not uncommon for children of parents with a mental illness. Anecdotal study points to instances where the pressure has led some children to commit crimes and go on to engage in risky behaviors. Like so many of those children, I was in an uphill battle to combat the toxic emotions and self-limiting thoughts. To begin, I had to stop comparing my life to that of others, even people who were a part of my extended family. After all, comparison is the quickest route to disappointment. There are often no signs letting you know you are headed there. Like a dead-end street, comparison leads us nowhere.

Even still, the pain of life had risen to a loud roar in my teenage years. It had become so loud that I thought my only option for relief was death. In hindsight, I would have done well to have a trusting adult figure to whom I could speak freely about my experiences at home. Though my grandmother served in such a capacity, there were unspoken limitations I had to adhere to. I can see how the presence of a trusted adult—a mentor, or a therapist—would have helped me process the questions.

Risking It All

Like most families where parental mental illness is present, financial insecurities exist. So, when these children seek alternative ways of securing their needs, it is, to few, a surprise. I almost fell into the trap of criminal activity but thank God for the bumblebee. Let me explain.

It was summer break from school, and the idea of working a summer job had been birthed in my mind after attending the Detroit Public Schools Compact Program presentation. A hiccup in completing the registration form had put in jeopardy my participation. So, what was I to do? I wanted to be able to purchase some fresh gear (clothes) for the summer and the upcoming school year. My small job at the local resale shop and cutting grass was not yielding enough to purchase all that I wanted.

In the neighborhood, I knew of young boys, and even some girls, who "hustled" to get the latest gear and swag. Thinking I could do it, I decided to talk to the neighborhood dope man about becoming one of "the boys." He actually laughed at me, but he told me to meet up with him later. My self-defeating and self-depleting thoughts were on replay, and the volume was loud. I made up my mind that I would work for him just to make some cash to buy the latest gym shoes—Nike Air Force Ones.

It was sunny and beautiful out that day, so bike riding was in order. Being secretive, I mounted my bike and told my granny I was going to the store. In actuality, I was going to go meet with the dope guy to get an assignment, *or so I thought*. Less than a block from the house, I paddled the fifteen-speed bike with no hands on the handlebars. With the wind in my face, I went underneath a low hanging tree branch. Immediately, I felt a sharp pain in the top, center of my head. Losing control of the bike, I went down like the Bronze Bomber, Deontay Wilder in his February 2020 fight against Tyson Fury. The next thing I remember is waking up at the hospital. My grandmother standing over me looked me in the face and said, "Whatever you were planning to do, you have betta thank God for the bumblebee."

While I was headed for trouble, the branch of the tree I had hit while riding disturbed a bee hive. The disturbance caused a bee to retaliate by stinging me in my head. What could have been the beginning of my criminal history report was extinguished by a bumblebee. I am thankful for the whole incident, as the experience provided me with tremendous protection.

Unfortunately, this is not always the outcome for children of parents with mental illness. Many are not as fortunate to have a bumblebee sting stop them from engaging in risky behaviors.

So, how do we help them?

We must engage in intentional wraparound services for families where mental illness exists. Engaging these children with positive caring adult mentors, teaching positive self-image and encouraging positive self-esteem to them are all avenues to reach them. This level of support, I believe, will help them process through the questions and confront their fears.

But more importantly, it will expend the toxic stress that sometimes comes with being the child of a parent with mental illness.

17 | THE NEED FOR RESILIENCE

Children are innately resilient—*or so I have been told*. They can oftentimes cope well with a myriad of life disruptions. This is especially true in instances where the disruption is short-lived and noncyclical. Even more, a child's chances of bouncing back from life's disruptions are increased when the child understands the *what* and *why* of the disruption. But what happens when a child is faced with long-term and cyclical disruptions for which they never understand the what or why? Is there hope for such a child? What protective measures could be taken to ensure that child's life success?

Children of parents with mental illness are not likely to be afforded the opportunity to endure short-term disruptions. On the contrary, these children, like myself, often face long-term and cyclical disruptions because of mental illness. Sustained homelessness, food insecurity, abuse and violence are typical disruptions faced by children living in the shadows of parental mental illness—especially in minority communities. Though parents and caregivers can do their best to prohibit, or at least limit, the impacts on a child, no child escapes unscathed.

So, what then is our answer?

According to research, three ways that adults and youth-serving systems can mitigate some of the trauma and stress [children] face, maximizing their emotional well-being: relationships, routine, and *resilience*. Relationships help develop self-esteem, confidence, and a sense of security. Routines increase feelings of emotional safety. *Resilience* allows one to move forward in the face of fallbacks and adversity (Whitfield, 2020).

Resilience: the ability to adapt and bounce back when we experience a difficult circumstance in life. It is our ability to recoil after life spreads us thin. Like a muscle that bounces back after being stretched, resilience is our ability to retake shape and move forward. For children of parents with mental illness, resilience is a *must*. In our holistic approach to treating parental mental illness, social service agencies and clinicians will do well to provide resilience training to children and other family members in the home.

It is true that, as we mature, our measure of resilience changes and develops. Like a muscle in the body, the more we exercise it, the greater its elasticity. Even still, teaching and training the mind to be resilient is no easy task, but it's not impossible. With the right support, as children encounter the diversity of life circumstances, they can develop resilience. Through exercises and therapy, children can learn how to cope—developing their own methods and mechanisms.

But the act of supporting a child requires us to know that child. One of the greatest failures I have observed in the social service sector has been agencies serving children they do not know. There is no one-size-fits-all approach when supporting children—and this cannot be truer for children living in the shadows of parental mental illness. To adequately serve a child in these living conditions, agencies must engage with the child on the ground level.

I could only have hoped for such an intense and intentional level of support from healthcare and social service professionals growing up. In the school of resilience, it was me, my grandmother and God. Granny taught me all she could about bouncing back from life's upsets. As a former sharecropper, housekeeper and cook in the racially divided south, she knew something about resilience. Yet, through all of her teaching—and dare I say, preaching—granny could not shield me from the painful disturbances of parental mental illness.

I thank God for His grace and my grandmother, who made it her business to build me up with her words, teaching me *resilience*.

18 | HEALNG FOR OUR WOUNDS

The healing of a wound takes treatment, time and covering. Yet, how does one receive healing for a wound that is not readily visible to the naked eye? This is perhaps the hardest of chapters to write for me because I am confronting a few wounds that, though years have passed, the pain is sometimes still felt.

Another question that plagues my mind is, "Whose fault was it that my mom has schizophrenia?" Over the years, the sting of this question has lessened, but the volume remains. I remain in wonderment as to the cause and onset of her mental illness. I am aware that *knowing* will not change anything. However, for me, it will be like finding the missing corner to the thousand-piece puzzle. The reality is this: when someone you love is hurting, you try your best to soothe them. And sometimes, you place unrealistic expectations upon yourself. At one point, I would even blame myself for her condition. If I could just behave better in school, or act appropriately in public settings, then she would get better.

It is not uncommon for children of parents with mental illness to feel this wide range of emotions. When a parent has a mental illness, children are vulnerable to the stigma and rejection, compounded by a lack of understanding from people at school and in the community. The limitations and fear of others can root a child to feeling isolated and cause them to withdraw from people. When a parent has a mental illness, them seeking and holding down a job might be difficult. The issue of unemployment, or under-employment, may lead to further problems for the family. This could put even more stress on children.

For the child in a home with parental mental illness, the stress of it all may result in the possibility of having troubles at school. There may be difficulties concentrating and the increased responsibilities at home will disturb sleep patterns. All of this can lead to a child feeling like they are not like other children. In hindsight, I recognize how fortunately blessed I was to have a grandmother, who reminded me almost daily that I was not responsible for causing my mom's mental illness. Even still, it did not get through to me as quickly as it should have. Throughout much of my teenage years, I struggled with feelings of shame, guilt and anger. I even went as far as trying to commit suicide, hoping to free myself from the pain of it all.

Yeah, I attempted suicide! I had become despondent, recluse and angry. When I recollect on that day, it was quite similar to all the others, except my desire to exit life was realized. I loathed my life! Honestly, nothing out of the ordinary was happening that had not already been occurring. But the pressure of my fragile life was getting the best of me. So, I thought to myself: *Why not ingest a mix of cleaning products and end my life?* And that's what I did. Only, not even suicide wanted me. The next morning, I woke up to my grandmother standing over me, telling me breakfast was ready. *Doggonit!* I thought to myself. *It didn't work!* Right, it *didn't.*

My mom's mental illness, coupled with an absent father, had me living a life of mental torment. I always felt like an outcast among people who I was told were related to me. Each of them had something that I envied. Height. Stamina. Skin tone. Courage. You name it, I envied them for it. Ultimately, this led to a poor self-image and self-hatred. I wanted so badly just to be a little faster. A little thinner. Okay, maybe *a lot thinner*. The brass tax was that I was unhappy with myself. And the more people I found myself around, the more I only felt worse. In each new person, I found something wrong in *me*. So, I grew reclusive and introverted. Puberty only made things worse. My first pimple made me hate my skin tone even more. In my mind, if I were of darker complexion, I could hide the big red zit that sat on my left cheek amidst the freckles. But for whatever reason, when the color codes were called for me at birth, someone was attracted to the lighter shades.

When I mentioned to a few of my family, friends and acquaintances that I was going to write this book, some paused and stared at me across the table or held the phone in silence. Some applauded the idea and gave pointers on what to include. Noting their care and concern for my wellbeing, I assured them that my intent was to help others.

In fact, the reason for sharing our story has never been to draw pity. Instead, my endeavor is to shed some light on the sometimes silent, unseen and burden bearers of parental mental illness. Until we talk about mental illness, the stigma will remain. But, one of my friend's voices cracked as he talked to me about his own childhood trauma.

As he shared about his upbringing and the mental toll it had taken on him, he paused and said, "I just want you to be alright after you start diving into this project." Admittedly, the process of writing this book has been a rollercoaster ride of emotions. On more than one occasion, I shelved the idea and went back to the daily routines. But inside, there remained a void. And the reminders to complete the project were there.

Sure, my life now is fair and good. And like most red-blooded humans, I have the daily struggles that follow the path of life. But all in all, I have no complaints. However, I would be remiss to not mention that the life I have now was not always in view. Some days, I cried, wondering if life would ever be for me what I had seen it be for others. I quickly learned that the vision we have in our heads does not always reach the surface of our realities. If they do, they arrive *distorted.*

But no worries. *I'm alright!*

No doubt, you've heard many people exclaim, "I'm alright!" Undoubtedly, they said it at the most inopportune time. Like the time when an aunt discovered a lump in her breast, but to preserve her superwoman perception, she responded, "I'm alright." Or the time when a college buddy learned the corporation was downsizing and his position was being phased out. Or perhaps it was the day you learned that your favorite flavor of ice cream was being discontinued at the local ice cream parlor. Arguably on opposite ends of the spectrum of importance, each occasion presented an emotion within us that warranted a response. For me, the response was, "I'm alright."

But was I *really*?

Growing up in a home with parental mental illness, I used the statement as a means to get people to leave me alone. I simply wanted the seclusion to process my thoughts—or ignore them if I chose to do so. In many instances, the two-word phrase became the decree of the day, no matter what occurred. Good, bad, ugly or indifferent, for me, "I'm alright" was my linguistical impromptu way of leaving the moment.

That phrase was my escape from the moment on that March morning in 1995, when I woke up to learn that my favorite aunt had been murdered in her home. Just hours before, I was scheduled to spend the night at her house. However, she changed her mind about having me stay overnight. She watched me through the small alleyway that separated 33rd from 32nd Street. I left her yard, closing the gate, and entered into my grandmother's yard as she yelled,

"See you later." On that faithful morning, I sat in the living room of our house, numb, filled with fear, anger and sadness.

My grandmother asked, "Tony, are you okay?"

In a stiff response, I said, "I'm alright." But I wasn't!

Behind those words was a great deal of angst, discomfort and, in that instance, just simple avoidance.

Fast forward twenty years later, when at twenty-nine years old, I sat in a courtroom, awaiting a judge to render a judgment of divorce. Those same words escaped through my lips into the ears of my attorney. That experience taught me that there remains so much behind those words for myself and others. "I'm alright" became the never-ending song, the radio version of my life's soundtrack. Unedited, unfiltered and *loud*! No matter what happened, those words remained my anthem—perhaps hoping that one day, I *really would be alright.*

So, you could imagine what my response was whenever our home life took a turn for the worse as a child. Yes, just like every bad day before, I walked around exclaiming to all that inquired, "I'm alright."

A Changed Perspective

I have come to the conclusion that we spend an inordinate amount of time, especially men, shielding ourselves from feeling the emotions, pain and dissatisfaction of situations that transpire in our lives. We create a façade, hoping to show the world just how strong we are. After all, we are taught to show no weakness. Young boys are consistently told to, "Man up!" and "You better not cry!" But thank God for brothers like Jason Wilson who told us we could *Cry Like a Man*. I have learned throughout the many life experiences that there is a great deal of strength in acknowledging our weaknesses. We all must discover that proper place to do so. We must seek a place of healing for our wounds.

In every instance that I share our story, I invite others into this place of healing and wholeness. Why? Because it does exist! It is a place, hidden from public view, where we can love ourselves unapologetically, laugh relentlessly, and cry profoundly. Although we cover up our emotions and avoid the feelings as to not appear weak and vulnerable to others, this place allows us to freely feel. Where is this mystical, perhaps even celestial place? It's a place in God where we learn to see ourselves and love ourselves just as He does.

I discovered this place through *therapy*.

19 | THERAPY HELPS!

As I sat in my therapist's office reciting the happenings of the recent months, I couldn't help but notice how negative I talked about myself. Everyone and everything were positive and uplifting, until it came to me. Finally, seemingly to get disgusted with my negative self-talk, my therapist asked, "Antoine, what *do* you *like* about you?"

Frozen in the moment and speechless, I couldn't answer.

Knowing that I am nowhere near perfect, it saddened me that I could not find anything to present in response to her question. The truth was that I was a twenty-five-year-old broken man. I had been weakened by repeated trauma and heartbreak. My dreams had turned into nightmares and visions had become distorted. As a result, I could no longer see the value of myself.

Through therapy over the course of a year and a half, I spent a great deal of time rediscovering me! Not to be cliché-ish, but I took myself out on dates, stood in the mirror studying my facial features, revisited vision statements and goals I had written—all in search of me! I understand this is uncommon for a man. My therapist told me so and she reminded me how difficult and rather taxing it would be.

It really was!

However, I forced myself not to fall prey to the societal pressure to hide what I felt because I am a man. While it can be said of both men and women, it is most notably observed that men are quick to use phrases like, "I'm alright" as a means of dismissing people when they get too close. In turn, what we do is become removed from our emotions and develop an inability to have healthy relationships with anyone—including our wives, children and families.

I drew strength from the Scriptures that gave examples of men who were mighty, yet they were unashamed to acknowledge their emotions. Paramount in the Scriptures is Jesus, who when hearing of His friend Lazarus' death, wept! This short verse in Scripture gave me insurmountable strength to keep moving forward. It also taught me an important lesson: your weeping doesn't mean you're a wimp.

I have since found great healing in sharing our story—and even the portions of it that involve only me. I hear countless others attest to how carelessly frequent they used the phrase, "I'm alright." Some have pulled me to the side, stating, "I've learned the two-word phrase as a quick way to relieve the pressure of someone inquiring about my wellbeing." My encouragement to us all is to leave that phrase and come into this place of safety where we can acknowledge our emotions and heal from the traumas we have endured.

Healing is what we should all desire to come away with after experiencing any trauma. To every young and adult child of a parent with mental illness: there is hope and healing for us. Even with the best of efforts to avoid them, we will all experience painful, traumatic events in our lives. However, we can survive those moments by taking on the mindset that, *I'm not alright at the moment, but I will be.*

Doing so will lead us to a place that we can boldly proclaim, "I'm alright."

20 | THIRTEEN LETTERS

As I grew to understand what the thirteen letters strung together meant, my heart sank for my mom. All those years, for what seemed like forever, my mom had been battling this internal war. Although I did not have the diagnosis, I knew how lonely I felt and I could only imagine how she must have felt. Like riding a roller coaster blindfolded, we could not see the twist and turns ahead. How were we going to help her? Would she survive this mental disorder? Could our family survive this mental disorder?

It is expected that some parents will try to protect their children from the burden of parental mental illness. One of the ways this happens is when parents attempt to keep it a secret or by making the topic unmentionable in the home. This does more harm than helping a child. While this may be done for good reasons, this is a blunder and can make it increasingly problematic for children to cope with parental mental illness. Being truthful with children about the conditions of their home empowers these children to cope and manage their emotions.

Truth is always the best response. Thankfully, my grandmother had the wisdom and know-how to provide me with age-appropriate dialogue about my mother's condition. Perhaps she understood that I already had a wide range of emotions and thoughts spiraling in my head. These thirteen letters birthed fear and worry within me. But her approach was beneficial to me, and it prepared me for the future that I now live in today.

A few months after graduating high school, I became the legal guardian of my mother, moving her and my brother into my home. Their daily care became my sole responsibility. I still wrestled with bouts of self-blame for my mother's illness, and this oftentimes led me to feeling depressed. To combat these episodic moments, I set out to learn more and more about the illness. I faced the fears head on that I may develop the same illness. Through research, I learned the truth about schizophrenia and mental illness. One of the most freeing enlightenments was that, although for some conditions, the risk of having similar illnesses can be higher within families. There were opportunities to reduce these risks in children. Understanding the illness helped me see there could be light at the end of the tunnel. Yet, I cautiously want you to be aware that, in some instances where children may receive all the right support and explanation, feelings of fear, fright, worry and shame of their parent's illness or behavior at times can arise.

21 | A NEW LEVEL OF CARE

Being the caregiver to a parent with mental illness comes with significant challenges. The responsibility to care for our loved ones seems to just to fall in our laps. The sometimes-unspoken expectations of others—and ourselves—makes us feel obligated to assume the responsibility for the care and welfare of our parent. For children of parents with mental illness, most of our stress comes from the unrealistic, unspoken and situational demands and expectations we, and sometimes others, burden us with. I know this all too well because this was my experience growing up and it all became realized in the months following my high school graduation.

After moving from the three-family unit following repeated disputes with the property owner, my grandmother moved us all into the three-bedroom home on 32nd street. Located one block over from the three-family unit, the move was not as traumatic as it could have been. My mom and brother remained in need of a caregiver; however, my mom's impatience began to get the best of her.

As my grandmother got older, the idea of leading a home with a teenager, developmentally impaired young adult, mentally impaired adult, and two young children (my cousins whose mom had been murdered) was next to impossible. Not to mention that mom's mental breaks grew again in frequency. The outbursts stemmed from her demands for independence and it became quite difficult for the family not to acquiesce. Following an outburst at the house, and later being petitioned into the local psychiatric hospital, my mom was discharged and moved in with her eldest sister. My brother and I remained with our grandmother, and my sister found escape with her new boyfriend.

Things seemed to settle for a while—but boy was it a short-lived while. My mother's incessant cries for independence and hallucinating rants grew louder. She demanded control of her finances and, when not heard, she'd enter into curse word-laden and property damaging episodes. Soon, the family decided to give in to her demands. No blame here, but it was not the best of moves for Mom. She began renting a home on the west side of Detroit, where she, along with my brother and sister, would live. The hiccups leading to her acquiring the property should have been tell-tell signs that this was not going to bid well.

The weeks leading up to Mom getting the keys were filled with a series of unfortunate events. For one, the house was broken into and became occupied by squatters—persons who illegally occupy an uninhabited building. When they finally left, the property was riddled with trash and graffiti painted on the walls. Still incessant about moving, Mom refused to delay the move-in. I remember my grandmother asking if I had planned to move with my mother. My answer was a resounding, "No!"

I did visit the house a few times. At each visit, I could see quickly the living conditions of the home beginning to enter the all-too familiar states I had experienced as a child. Small carpet stains had gone untreated and uncleaned, and now required replacement. Dishes remained in the sink for weeks. The stench in the uncleaned bathroom was all too familiar and a disconcertingly reminder that Mom was in no way ready to lead a home. My brother and sister resided in the house, but even their presence in the home did little to stave off the inevitable.

One day after arriving home from school, I heard my grandmother on the phone discussing who I knew could only be my mom. "They don't have no water in that house," she said. "We will fill some jugs with water and take them over." My aunt arrived a few hours later and we loaded the recycled jugs we had filled with water in the car. When we arrived, my brother met us at the door with no shirt on, and the voice of my mother was yelling from the house. The grass had grown high and the rising temperatures caused the stench from the house to meet you at the steps. My aunt demanded they turn on a fan and open a window. Entering the house with jugs of water in hand, I could see that my mom had made some small attempts to straighten up. My grandmother ordered me into the bathroom, saying, "Boy, go pour three of these in that toilet and flush it." As I did, the soiled toilet water splattered up on my pants and I could have died. The home's conditions had become unbearable, as Mom seldom cleaned and took care of the house.

Driving away from the house, I remember thinking to myself, "Who is going to fix this?"

As if she was in my head, my grandmother said, "Tony, you're going to have to take care of your mom and brother." A junior in high school, my focus had begun to shift to what life could be like for me after graduation. So, her words immediately caused an internal conflict. Those questions from years earlier had come back like hurricane waters breaking the levy. My soul was flooding at the thought of having to assume responsibility for my mom and brother right after high school. But the reality was there was no one else to do it.

A few months prior to graduating from high school, my grandmother had begun showing signs of what we later learned was dementia. Our talks that I had grown accustomed to had grown thin. Though still physically active, her mind was gradually stalling. She was forgetting things, people and names. Though, she had always called us grandkids by differing names—mixing us up. But her misfiring's were noticeable, and my heart was breaking as I watched my saving grace battle to remember details. After coming home one evening, she stopped sewing a blouse to say to me that I needed to put together a plan to help my mom because the situation at the house was not getting better. It seemed like the dementia was gone, and the magnificent lady who had cared for me all these years was back. In what seemed like an hours-long conversation, she poured out wisdom, telephone numbers and instructions on how to go about it.

The week of my graduation was pretty busy. Picking up my suit, getting a haircut and pleading for my mom to attend were the smaller matters at hand. Larger than all of that was the discussions I was having with a local realty company about a property one block over from my grandmother. It was a nice three-bedroom ranch home. It seemed perfect for my family. Prior to graduation, I had pretty much made up my mind that it was best for me to forgo going away for college. Instead, I was going to stay home to care for my mother and brother. A decision that, until this day, I question.

After receiving my diploma just weeks earlier, I was now moving into a new home with my mom and brother, assuming full responsibility for their care. Each of us had our own room, something we had not experienced before whenever we were in the same house. That summer was pretty uneventful. Mom adjusted to the move because it was in the same neighborhood as the house she had rented. Her frequent trips to the store were not interrupted and she could always stop by granny's house, who was just a block over. That fall, I had made my final decision to stay home and not go away for college—to the disappointment of many.

Determined to still go to college, I enrolled at University of Detroit Mercy and began taking classes. At the same time, I was employed at a local credit union—all the while being caregiver and legal guardian of my mother and brother. The deck was stacked pretty high. Going to class, work and coming home to prepare meals and clean had become the consistent flow for me. Not to mention, I had decided to get married at the ripe age of eighteen. That is for an entirely different book.

Attempting to manage it all, I flunked out of college after one semester, losing a pretty lucrative scholarship. Probably more detrimental, I lost the desire for higher education.

I soon learned that every decision I made had to have the propensity to affect the broader spectrum of my mother's and brother's health. Even when I sought out professional in-home care for them, it often paled in comparison to the level of care I thought they needed—and that I so desperately wanted to provide for them. After speaking with a social work from the local Health and Human Services office, she kindly explained to me that professional home-care services can never be compared to that of care provided by a family. Therefore, my focus had to be on being an advocate for them as they received care from professionals.

22 | ENDINGS AND NEW BEGINNINGS

Mental illness, unlike other diseases, is not always visible. Because of this, people suffer in isolation and silence. In many instances, the suffering is not relegated only to the patient, but to those who provide their care. Thankfully, advances in healthcare and treatment options are allowing patients and caregivers to effectively manage mental illness. This improving state of care is enhancing the quality of life of the care receiver and the caregiver.

For our family, coupled with professional support, and the oversight of medical professionals, we've been on a pretty steady course for the past five or so years. My mother's daily care is now in the hands of trained professionals with me actively engaged as her legal guardian, but more importantly as an advocate. Mom resides in a residential facility that affords her the amenities, care and freedom to live her best life. She is actively participating in day programs that allow her to learn and hone new skills. She travels periodically and she is kept active. All of the experiences we have had caused my love to grow stronger over the years. I enjoy speaking to her by phone and our interactions usually end in a smile, laughs or an I love you!

So, the idea of moving Mom into such a facility at first, I must admit, was challenging for me. However, the demands of my immediate family and my career have increased over the years and warranted a change. Grasping how my mother's mental health condition inevitably placed me, her child, in the anticipated role of a caregiver, I had to prepare myself to make some tough decisions. Each decision marked an ending, but also a new beginning for us.

I am sure that the feelings and emotions I experience are not unique to me. As the son of a mother with schizophrenia, I have grappled with a myriad of emotions—but none more than the emotion of *fear of the future*. The roller coaster-like twists and turns that come with parental mental illness have the proclivity to leave you on edge, wondering what's next. And this does not go away when you—the child—become an adult. For me, it increased in occurrences. So how do we combat these emotions that can send us into a tailspin?

A man of faith, I had to receive that, *God has not given us the spirit of fear; but of power, and of love, and of a sound mind* (2 Timothy 1:7, KJV). To maintain my personal mental health in the face of parental mental illness, I have to remember that I have *"power, love* and *a sound mind"*. These three ingredients, when mixed with action, become the secret sauce of survival for children—or anyone—providing care to someone with a mental illness. But how does this look in our everyday lives?

The *power* is observed in our lives when we take authority over the portions that we can control. An example in my life was the day I decided to legally pursue guardianship of my mother. For years, I watched as my grandmother and aunts struggled to get help and treatment for my mother. After one of her paranoid hallucinations, they would petition her into a facility, only for her to sign herself out two or three days later. Of course, she was still in no condition to move forward. But the legal rights to sign herself out of care overruled my grandmother's desires. Someone had to take the power and use it for the betterment of her life. So, I did.

The *love* is observed in our decisions. Seems pretty straightforward, but allow me to illuminate for you why you are doing what you are doing for your loved one. Every time you make a decision to encourage and support your loved one in managing their mental illness, you are operating in a place of love. Love is an action word. It is the driving force behind our decisions to seek out resources—even when faced with the greatest of difficulties. Love keeps us going.

Then, there is the *sound mind*. Perhaps more important to us than anything is our ability to remain in soundness of mind. That is key to our success. Maintaining our own mental health is essential in helping our loved ones survive mental illness. Sometimes in our desperation to heal our loved ones, we lose control and give in to our emotions, causing us to act out and do things that we ordinarily would not do. We must strive to remain sound in our minds—and prayer helps me to do that. Below is a prayer I often pray when times get tough and emotions start to get the best of me.

Dear Lord,

I thank you for life, for that of my mother and brother. I realize that you are the giver and sustainer of life. For that, I am thankful. Lord, I ask that you grant me to know the peace that comes from you and you alone. Give me to know your peace according to John 14:27.

Guide me as I provide care for my mother and brother, preparing their meals, managing their finances, and advocating for their care. Fill my heart with love and devotion for their lives. Grant me patience and understanding when things are done or said that hurt my feelings. Lord, strengthen my mind to endure the stress and give me wisdom to know when to seek respite.

Father, I pray for each medical, mental health and social service employee who shall come in contact with my mom and brother. Remove all malicious and mischievous motives and actions. Give them an honest tongue and pure intentions. Help me to know when to challenge treatment recommendations and when to trust their professional opinions. Provide me with knowledge on how to better care for my mother and brother.

Finally, Lord, help me to stand up against bias, stigma and injustice against my mom and others who face mental illness. Remind me of your loving strength when the weight of the matter gets too heavy. Bless and keep my mother and brother. In Jesus' name. Amen!

A LETTER TO CAREGIVERS:

Re: At the Intersection of Faith, Hope & Love

Dear Caring One,

First, let me say how brave I think you are! I commend your readiness to face the uncertainties of caring for a loved one—whether they are facing mental illness or physical illness. I have lived your reality and experienced the pressure of the moments. The sleepless nights, the endless appointments, and the need to keep a tedious schedule are not foreign to me by far. I recognize that your devotion to your loved one keeps you showing up. But allow me to be honest and say that there will be some days that even our devotion won't feel like enough. Our souls and our bodies will become depleted of energy, and our minds work by the constant need to be "on" at all times. Our finances will become stretched. Our commitments to ourselves and friends will become strained. Even our own health suffers. All while we are attempting to give care to those whom we love.

So, what do we do when the care we give becomes a heavier load for us to bear? From where do we draw strength? When the circumstances of our lives have become distorted, how do we find a clearer picture? For me, it was at the intersection!

The intersection of faith, hope and love! Perhaps not a physical location, this intersection became the source of strength during those days when life seemed too hard to get out of bed. Or like the day my mom wandered off from the house and spent the weekend traversing the late-March winter streets of Detroit before being found by a vigilant resident. This intersection has become the place of my strength. This is the place that helps me survive the ominous shadows cast by mental illness.

It is in this place that I invite you to come. Bring your faith in God, your hope for the future, and your love for your loved one. Here you can lay down the superhero cape and don only the feelings of your heart. Through prayer, may you receive the strength of God and the peace that He promises to give. I pray you divulge all your cares here and remember them only as things you have given to God.

Be encouraged in knowing that your labor of love is not unnoticed—even when earthly persons cannot mention it. Like a sweet-smelling savor in the nostrils, so is your caregiving to the Father above. He is not slack to forget, and He will reward you.

God bless you and your family as you travel this path of life, facing the distorted realities with truth and light.

Antoine

EPILOGUE:
HEALTH DISPARITIES IN BLACK-MINORITY AND LOW-INCOME COMMUNITIES IN THE UNITED STATES

Health disparities in the United States can be measured by the prevalence, incidence, mortality and morbidity of particular populations due to pre-existing health determinants. Based on the data from Healthy People 2020, the black-minority and low-income communities record the highest cases of health disparities as a result of the racial difference and socioeconomic status (Barr, 2014). Their vulnerability comes from exposure to risk factors such as inaccessibility to quality healthcare, non-affordability of care services, low health literacy levels, and cultural influences and beliefs. The healthcare resources and facilities in the regions populated by these vulnerable populations are inadequate to meet the population needs and don't meet the standards of quality care (Barr, 2014).

Therefore, most of them end up succumbing to diseases that could be managed with better facilities or attentiveness.

The historical policies, social perceptions and prevailing practices have a continual effect on the administration of the care to blacks in the United States. Most cases of negligence and discrimination due to skin color have been reported in the majority of the states and has contributed to the high morbidity and mortality rate in the black community (Barr, 2014). African-Americans have difficulties in being incorporated into the corporate world due to the social perceptions of their Caucasian counterparts. This aspect has contributed to the high unemployment rate in the black community. The majority of the African-American youth engaging in substance use, criminality and unhealthy lifestyles have been attributed to their idleness.

The malnutrition and exposure to harsh weather conditions for the low-income populations contribute to their high morbidity and mortality rates. They are not able to afford a balanced diet or even a decent meal for the day; therefore, their immune systems become weak and unable to fight diseases (Purnell, et al., 2016). Upon admission to hospitals, they are unable to pay for quality medical services and, therefore, end up waiting longer to receive substandard care, which exposes them to more risks of disease prevalence. The gap between the rich and the poor in the United States is increasingly growing, which puts the vulnerable populations at more risks of discrimination and inaccessibility to quality care (Purnell, et al., 2016). These populations' literacy levels and religious/cultural beliefs diminish their engagement to personal management and compliance with healthcare directives. It becomes difficult for them to apply good health practices that would enhance their quality of life and attain mental and physical health.

It is high time these systemic and structural issues that disproportionately affect black communities are addressed. Not with rhetoric and lip service but with actionable plans that include divestment in failing systems and investment into innovative and new systems.

HELP FOR MENTAL ILLNESS

National Suicide Prevention Lifeline

Call 1-800-273-TALK (8255); En Español 1-888-628-9454

The Lifeline is a free, confidential crisis hotline that is available to everyone 24 hours a day, seven days a week. The Lifeline connects callers to the nearest crisis center in the Lifeline national network. These centers provide crisis counseling and mental health referrals. People who are deaf, hard of hearing, or have hearing loss can contact the Lifeline via TTY at 1-800-799-4889.

Crisis Text Line

Text "HELLO" to 741741

The Crisis Text hotline is available 24 hours a day, seven days a week throughout the U.S. The Crisis Text Line serves anyone, in any type of crisis, connecting them with a crisis counselor who can provide support and information.

Veterans Crisis Line

Call 1-800-273-TALK (8255) and press 1 or text to 838255

The Veterans Crisis Line is a free, confidential resource that connects veterans 24 hours a day, seven days a week with a trained responder. The service is available to all veterans, even if they are not registered with the VA or enrolled in VA healthcare. People who are deaf, hard of hearing, or have hearing loss can call 1-800-799-4889.

Disaster Distress Helpline

Call 1-800-985-5990 or text "TalkWithUs" to 66746

The Disaster Distress Helpline provides immediate crisis counseling for people who are experiencing emotional distress related to any natural or human-caused disaster. The helpline is free, multilingual, confidential and available 24 hours a day, seven days a week.

Contact social media outlets directly if you are concerned about a friend's social media updates **or dial 911 in an emergency**

CITED REFERENCES

1987 - 2016 Yearly Homicide Totals. (2016). Retrieved
December 5, 2019, from
https://detroitmi.gov/document/1987-2016-yearly-
homicide-totals

Allen, L. (2015, July 23). Child Development and Early
Learning - Transforming the Workforce for
Children Birth Through Age 8 - NCBI Bookshelf.
Retrieved from
https://www.ncbi.nlm.nih.gov/books/NBK310550/

Barr, D. A. (2014). Health disparities in the United States:
Social class, race, ethnicity, and health. JHU Press.

Defining Quality of Life in the Children of Parents With
Severe Mental Illness: A Preliminary Stakeholder-
Led Model. (2013, September 10). Retrieved from
https://pubmed.ncbi.nlm.nih.gov/24040050/

Family Functioning and Psychological Health of Children
with Mentally Ill Parents. (2019, April 1). Retrieved
from
https://www.ncbi.nlm.nih.gov/pmc/articles/PMC64
79670/

Franklin, S. C. T. (2018, September 3). MURDERS TORMENT DETROIT. Retrieved August 8, 2019, from https://www.chicagotribune.com/news/ct-xpm-1987-01-13-8701040022-story.html

Hundreds of thousands of Michigan residents lack behavioral health treatment. (2019, July 30). Retrieved from https://mihealthfund.org/hundreds-of-thousands-lack-behavioral-health-treatment

Identification of Children of Parents With Mental Illness: A Necessity to Provide Relevant Support. (2020, June 9). Retrieved from https://www.ncbi.nlm.nih.gov/pmc/articles/PMC6333019/

Intermittent explosive disorder - Symptoms and causes. (2018, September 19). Retrieved March 6, 2020, from https://www.mayoclinic.org/diseases-conditions/intermittent-explosive-disorder/symptoms-causes/syc-20373921

M.D., S. L. C. (2018). Mayo Clinic Family Health Book 5th Edition: Completely Revised and Updated (5th ed.). Rochester, MN: Mayo Clinic Press.

Music therapy for people with schizophrenia and schizophrenia-like disorders. (2017). Retrieved from

https://www.cochranelibrary.com/cdsr/doi/10.1002/
14651858.CD004025.pub4/full#:~:text=Moderate%
E2%80%90%20to%20low%E2%80%90quality%20
evidence,schizophrenia%20or%20schizophrenia%E
2%80%90like%20disorders.

Poor school performance in offspring of patients with
schizophrenia: What are the mechanisms? (2012,
January 1). Retrieved from
https://www.ncbi.nlm.nih.gov/pmc/articles/PMC36
58106/

Purnell, T. S., Calhoun, E. A., Golden, S. H., Halladay, J.
R., Krok-Schoen, J. L., Appelhans, B. M., &
Cooper, L. A. (2016). Achieving health equity:
closing the gaps in health care disparities,
interventions, and research. Health Affairs, 35(8),
1410-1415.

Schizophrenia - Symptoms and causes. (2020, January 7).
Retrieved from
https://www.mayoclinic.org/diseases-
conditions/schizophrenia/symptoms-causes/syc-
20354443

Supplemental Security Income. (2020). Retrieved June 3,
2020, from https://www.ssa.gov/ssi/

The American Academy of Child and Adolescent

Psychiatry (AACAP). (2015, March). Mental Illness in Families. Retrieved from https://www.aacap.org/AACAP/Families_and_Yout h/Facts_for_Families/FFF-Guide/Children-Of-Parents-With-Mental-Illness-039.aspxinc

Toxic Stress. (2018, October 23). Retrieved October 11, 2019, from https://developingchild.harvard.edu/science/key-concepts/toxic-stress/

Whitfield, T. (2020, May 20). Michigan Chronicle. Retrieved from https://michiganchronicle.com/2020/05/20/caring-for-our-kids-during-covid-19/#/?playlistId=0&videoId=0

ACKNOWLEDGEMENTS

To God be the glory! All praise belongs to you. I am an awe of your willingness to use me as a vessel on the earth. Though flawed, you love me, anyway. When I fail, you lovingly receive me back through repentance and cleansing by the shed blood of Jesus Christ. Thank you for giving me life, and the opportunity to walk this path. Lord, I thank you! "To the only wise God our Savior, be glory and majesty, dominion and power, both now and ever. Amen." (Jude 25, KJV)

Writing a book has never been a solo or siloed process. Everyone in your life becomes a part of the process—knowingly or unknowingly to them.

As I consider the depth to which I had to reach to write this book, I am thankful for my mother. Her courageous strength is what inspires me to keep going. When I began this journey in 2016, her only advice was to, "Share enough to help someone."

To my wife, Kassandra, and my daughter, Madison: thank you for loving me enough to allow me time to process my thoughts, capture them on paper, and get this manuscript completed. Your love and devotion are appreciated. I love you and thank you for loving me.

To my late grandmother, Marie Rosco (1926-2009), your shoulders bore the brunt of my mother's illness for years. You remained strong, tenacious and committed to seeing us through. Selfishly, I like to think that all those years of teaching were preplanned. Maybe you knew that I would become legal guardian and caregiver of my mother and brother. Whatever the case, thank you! Your voice rings still in the hallways of my mind.

To my siblings Jeffrey and Kyra, you both have your own stories to share about our experience. Thank you for supporting and trusting me to detail a portion of our life that impacts us all. To extended family, my maternal aunts, uncle and cousins. Your encouragement to proceed with the book was mind-blowing. Each of you provided details about my mom that, without them, would have left the book vacant of vital details.

Ethan B. Sheard: My pops, you have been a great mentor,

friend, and confidant throughout this journey. My mom loves to hear your voice. Thank you for receiving me and my family into yours. Special shout out to Gwenda and Madison for allowing me to share in life with your family. God has blessed me because of you all.

ABOUT THE AUTHOR

ANTOINE D. JACKSON is a minister, author and entrepreneur. He has been described as an advocate, social innovator and strategist working in the nonprofit sector. His fifteen years of experience working in youth development, coupled with his personal life shines through his numerous literary projects.

He is a graduate of the University of Phoenix where he studied business administration. Antoine was named a Michigan Chronicle 40 Under 40, Church of God in Christ (COGIC) Achiever 20 under 40 and recipient of the University of Phoenix Spirit of Service award. Antoine serves as an Associate Elder at Greater Mitchell Temple Church of God in Christ. He has been entrusted with the youth ministry and leading outreach efforts by his pastor, Bishop John Henry Sheard.

Antoine has been a featured speaker at a variety of influential churches, events, universities and conferences. He is founder and host of *Flip the Switch Conference*, an annual empowerment conference held in Detroit.

Antoine is the proud husband to Kassandra Lynn and doting father a daughter, Madison, they reside in Detroit.

Learn more by visiting www.AntoineJackson.org.